LONGSIGHT THEATRE

WHERE DO LITTLE BIRDS GO?

Written by
CAMILLA WHITEHILL

Where Do Little Birds Go?

This version of the play was first performed at
Camden People's Theatre in August 2014.

It went on to be performed at VAULT Festival in February 2015 where it won the People's Choice Award, before embarking on a UK tour. In August 2015 the play enjoyed a critically acclaimed, sell-out run at the Underbelly Cowgate, Edinburgh Festival Fringe 2015, with the TIMES hailing it a 'low-key triumph'. It was subsequently picked up by The Old Red Lion Theatre for a month-long London transfer run in November 2016.

Cast and creative team as follows:

Cast: **Jessica Butcher**

Writer – **Camilla Whitehill**
Director – **Sarah Meadows**
Producer – **Rosalyn Newbery**
Designer – **Justin Nardella**
Associate Designer – **Catherine Morgan**
Lighting Designer – **Jamie Platt**
Composer and Sound Designer – **Benedict Taylor**

PR – **Chloe Nelkin Consulting**
Graphic Design – **Rebecca Pitt**

Presented by Longsight Theatre
www.longsighttheatre.com

For more information about this production,
please visit www.longsighttheatre.com,
and follow us on Twitter at @LongsightTC and @LittleBirdsGo

ABOUT THE AUTHOR
Camilla Whitehill

Born in London and raised in Hastings, Camilla originally trained as an actor at the Birmingham School of Acting. She is one of six writers on the Bush Theatre emerging writers scheme, and was recently one of twelve writers part of the Channel 4 4Screenwriting programme. She has had short plays staged at the Royal Court, Soho Theatre, Southwark Playhouse, Arcola Theatre, New Diorama, and the Paines Plough Roundabout. Her award-winning debut play, *Where Do Little Birds Go?*, enjoyed a sell-out run at the Underbelly as part of Edinburgh Fringe 2015 ("A writer of huge promise...a low key triumph" The Times). Her second play *Mr Incredible* is published by Nick Hern and enjoyed a critically acclaimed run at the Underbelly as part of Edinburgh Fringe 2016, and is currently being developed for television. Her collaboration with Strictly Arts Theatre, *Freeman*, ran at the Belgrade Theatre, Coventry, in September 2016. It is currently being developed for a U.K. tour. Her personal storytelling project, *On The Crest Of A Wave*, will be at Vault Festival in February 2017. She lives in North London with her two cats, Buffy and Angel.

www.camillawhitehill.co.uk

***Lucy Fuller* – Jessica Butcher**
Jessica trained at Drama Studio London.

Since graduating in 2013 Jessica has played Lucy Fuller in *Where Do Little Birds Go?* firstly at the Camden People's Theatre, followed by a UK Tour and then at the Edinburgh Festival in 2015.

Other theatre includes: Fadia in *Saviour* (for 'A Night for Syria' at Theatre 503 & Vault Festival); Ella in *Scandinavia* (Leicester Square Theatre); Ariadne in *Live, Revive Lament* (UK Tour); Pat Milligan in London Wall (Tristan Bates); Bianca in *The Taming of the Shrew* (C Main, Edinburgh); Viola in *Twelfth Night* (The Nursery Theatre); Charlotte in *Party Time* (European Tour); Chorus in *Antigone* (Southwark Playhouse); Amanda in *Sometimes Looking Up* (Union Theatre) and Time in *The Winter's Tale* (Old Fire Station, Oxford).

Film and TV includes: Actor for the BBC EastEnders Directors Training scheme 2016. Singer in *Vivaldi's Women* (BBC) and Elizabeth Taylor in *The First Kiss* (Crescent Arts).

Director – Sarah Meadows
Sarah is an award winning director and Co-Artistic Director of Longsight Theatre Company. Recent credits include: *Home Is…*, Tolu Agbelusi & Apples and Snakes, UK tour; Contact Theatre, Manchester & Rich Mix, London, 2016; *Screwed* by Kathryn O'Reilly, Theatre 503 June/July 2016 (nominated for Off-West End Award for Best Director); *The Very Perry Show* by Kate Perry, San Francisco International Arts Festival, May/June 2016; *Where Do Little Birds Go?* by Camilla Whitehill, UK tour, VAULT Festival & Underbelly, Edinburgh Fringe Festival 2015, Old Red Lion Theatre 2016 (People's Choice Award, Vault Festival 2015); *Mr Incredible* by Camilla Whitehill, VAULT, February 2016 and Edinburgh Fringe 2016, (winner of the Origins

Award for Outstanding New Work 2016); *You* by Mark Wilson, Brighton Fringe 2015 (Argus Angel Award, Brighton Fringe Award For Theatre, The Fringe Review Outstanding Theatre Award). In development and staged readings: *Nadya*, by Chris Dury (with actors Michelle Terry and Stephen Tomkinson) The Park Theatre; *Texas Taxman* (Comedy), Luke Courtier, Arcola Theatre/VAULT Festival 2017; *On the Crest of a Wave*, Camilla Whitehill, VAULT Festival 2017. She is represented by Colin Blumenau, The Production Exchange Management.

Producer – Rosalyn Newbery
Rosalyn is a Theatre Producer who has worked extensively across theatre, live events and TV. She is Co-Artistic Director and Executive Producer with Longsight Theatre, Company Producer with Flipping the Bird and Associate Producer with *VAULT Festival*, Theatre Uncut and Look Left Look Right (LLLR). Recent theatre work: *Where Do Little Birds Go?* by Camilla Whitehill (Longsight Theatre: Old Red Lion Theatre London 2016, Underbelly Cowgate, Edinburgh Festival Fringe 2015); *The Eulogy of Toby Peach* by Toby Peach (UK Tour 2016/17, VAULT Festival 2016, Underbelly Cowgate, Edinburgh Festival 2015); *TORCH* by Phoebe Eclair-Powell (Flipping the Bird: Theatre Diorama, Underbelly Cowgate, Edinburgh Festival 2016, Latitude); *Mr Incredible* by Camilla Whitehill (Longsight Theatre: Underbelly Cowgate Edinburgh Festival Fringe, VAULT Festival 2016); VAULT Festival 2016 (Vaults, Waterloo); *Howard Barker Double Bill* (REND Productions: Arcola Theatre); *Vanity Bites Back* (UK tour, Edinburgh Festival 2015, VAULT 2015); *VAULT Festival 2015* (Vaults Waterloo); *Theatre Uncut Flagship Plays* (Young Vic, Traverse, UK tour); *The Bread + The Beer* (Solar Productions: 2014 UK tour); *The Itinerant Music Hall* (Flipping the Bird: Lyric Hammersmith, Watford Palace, GDIF, Latitude); *HEIST* (Theatre Delicatessen); *My Dear I Wanted to Tell You* (LLLR: Soho Theatre and site-specific); *You Once Said Yes* (LLLR: Perth International Arts Festival 2014, Edinburgh British Council Showcase 2013); *Once Upon A Christmas* (LLLR: Covent Garden); *The Many Whoops of Whoops Town* (LLLR: Lyric Hammersmith); *Come Heavy Sleep* (Kiln Ensemble: The REP Birmingham); *Eat Your Heart Out* (Kiln Ensemble: site-specific). Rosalyn also produces The London, Amsterdam and New York Coffee Festivals and has worked on TV series' for the BBC.

Designer – Justin Nardella

Justin's passion for the performing and visual arts led him to study theatre design at the National Institute of Dramatic Arts, Sydney, where he graduated in 2008. Theatre shows include: Gordon Frost Organisation: *Legends!*, Longsight Theatre, *Where Do Little Birds Go?* (Camden People's Theatre, VAULT Festival, UK Tour, Edinburgh Fringe 2015, Old Red Lion Theatre 2016), Longsight Theatre: *Mr Incredible* (Underbelly Edinburgh Fringe 2016, VAULT Festival 2016), Opera in Space: *Hansel and Gretel*, Brisbane Festival: *Tender Napalm* and *L'Orfeo*, Ensemble Theatre: *Circle Mirror Transformation*, Sydney Theatre Company: *Before and After*, Downstairs Belvoir: *Ladybird, Bliss and Whore*, Darlinghurst Theatre Co.: *Macbeth and Glace Chase*, Griffin Theatre Co.: *Porn. Cake and Silent Disco. Disco*, NORPA: *Engine*. Glent Street Theatre: *Every Single Saturday the Musical.* He is the Associate Set Designer on various international productions of *Priscilla Queen of the Desert* The Musical, was Associate Designer to Anish Kapoor on *Tristan and Isolde* (ENO) and to *King Lear* (The Old Vic). He was a site designer on Brisbane Festival where he designed and directed the 2011 program launch - which involved 4 semi trailers. For film he was the production designer on the IRIS short film *Spoilers* (Wales BAFTA Nomination Best Short Film), *Andy X* and The Scare's *Could Be Bad* music video. He has designed events for major brands including Audi, GHD and Aveda. He was the inaugural winner of the Australian BMW Young Artist of the Year Award.

Associate Designer – Catherine Morgan

Catherine trained at Nottingham Trent University. Design credits include: *Mr Incredible* (Underbelly Edinburgh Fringe 2016, VAULT Festival 2016), *Screwed* (Theatre 503), *Diaboliad* (Courtyard Theatre), *My Story, Rise and Fall, Ring of Envy and Verona Road* (Intermission Youth Theatre), *Twelfth Night* (New Wimbledon Theatre Studio), *Othello* (The Bussey Building), *Eisteddfod* (Latitude Festival for High Tide), *Baba Shakespeare* (RSC Courtyard Theatre, Arcola Theatre) *Gerbils in a Glass Cage* (The Space), *Fit for Purpose* (Pleasance, Edinburgh Festival) and *Macbeth* and *Hobson's Choice*. Associate design credits include: *I Puritani* (Welsh National Opera) and *Dido & Aeneas / La Voix Humaine* (Opera North). Catherine has acted as assistant to several leading designers including: Leslie Travers, Giles Cadle, Stewart Laing, Tom Cairns, Soutra Gilmour, Thaddeus

Strassberger, Helen Goddard, Ben Stones and Tim Goodchild. Recent assistant credits include *La Boheme* (The Royal Opera House), *The Hairy Ape* (The Old Vic, Park Avenue Armoury; New York) and *The Marriage of Figaro* (Kansas City Opera). Catherine works regularly with the National Theatre to develop and deliver workshops in theatre design aimed at young people.

Lighting Designer – Jamie Platt
Jamie trained at the Royal Welsh College of Music & Drama. He was nominated for an Off-West End Award in 2015 and in 2013 was the recipient of the Association of Lighting Designers' ETC Award and the Philip & Christine Carne Prize from RWCMD. Lighting designs include: *To Dream Again* (Clwyd Theatr Cymru), *Klippies* (Southwark Playhouse), *P'yongyang, We Know Where You Live, Chicken Dust* (Finborough Theatre), *Pattern Recognition* (Platform Theatre), *Screwed, Grey Man* (Theatre 503), *Constellations* (Théâtre Municipal de Fontainebleau), *Closer to Heaven* (Union Theatre), *Mahmud íle Yezida, BOY, Misbehaving, The Intruder, Bald Prima Donna, The Red Helicopter* (Arcola Theatre), *And Now: The World!* (Derby Theatre & UK Tour), *Make/Believe* (V&A Museum), *Ring The Changes+* (Southbank Centre), *The Marriage of Figaro* (Kirklinton Hall, Carlisle & UK Tour), *Neverland, One Thousand + 1, Fellini: Book of Dreams, AnneX, QuiXote, Due Saponette Rosse di Tritolo, BURN* (Fucecchio, Italy), *Romeo & Juliet* (Pleasance Theatre), *Feed, Boat* (Platform Arts Hub), *The Eulogy of Toby Peach* (The Vaults, UK Tour), *Mr. Incredible* (The Vaults & Underbelly, Edinburgh), *MICROmegas* (Riverside Studios), *Grimm Tales* (John Lyon Theatre), *Arthur's Quest* (V45, Edinburgh), *The Children's Hour, Earthquakes in London, Arabian Nights* (Bute Theatre), *Once a Catholic, The Merchant of Venice* (Richard Burton Theatre), *Merrily He Rolls Along, Honk!, Footloose* (Epsom Playhouse). As Associate Lighting Designer: Imogen (Shakespeare's Globe), *The Grit in the Oyster* (Sadler's Wells & World Tour), *The Measures Taken, All That Is Solid Melts Into Air* (Linbury Studio, Royal Opera House & World Tour), *Our Big Land* (New Wolsey Theatre & UK Tour), *The Buskers Opera* (Park Theatre), *Don Giovanni* (West Road Concert Hall, Cambridge).

Composer and Sound Designer – Benedict Taylor

Benedict Taylor is an award winning composer & solo violist specialising in contemporary music and improvisation. He studied at the Royal Northern College of Music & Goldsmiths College, and is a leading figure within the area of contemporary composition & string performance, at the forefront of the British & European new and improvised music scene. He composes, performs & records internationally, in many leading venues and festivals including: Royal Court Theatre, Rambert Dance Company, BBC Arts Online, Berlinale, Venice International Film Festival, BFI London Film Festival, Toronto Film Festival, Huddersfield Contemporary Festival, London Contemporary Music Festival, Aldeburgh Festival, Cantiere D'Arte di Montepulciano, Edinburgh Festival, CRAM Festival, Cafe Oto, The Barbican, Royal Albert Hall, Southbank Centre, The Vortex, Ronnie Scott's, ICA, BBC Radio 3 and 2, Radio Libertaire Paris, Resonance FM London. Through his work he is involved with a number of higher education institutions, giving composition, improvisation & performance lectures at the Royal College of Music and Goldsmiths College, amongst others. He is the founder and artistic director of CRAM, a music collective and independent record label dedicated to new music.

Longsight Theatre

Longsight Theatre makes award-winning, brave, intimate theatre with a focus on new writing.

www.longsighttheatre.com

FOREWORD FROM THE WRITER

I wrote the first draft of this play over three years ago. It was my first full length play, the first proper play I ever had on, my first published book, my first big reviews. It got me my agent and most of my subsequent jobs. I love this play, but it makes me sad. It makes me sad because the themes in this play - sexual exploitation, assault, and rape – are more prevalent than ever today. And this play is set in the fucking Sixties. In Lucy we have an imperfect victim – a provocative, sexual woman, who makes mistakes – exactly the kind of assault victim we rake over the coals today.

I'm writing this a few days after Ched Evans' successful appeal, when there are men and women online calling his victim a slut and a whore with such undisguised glee it makes my skin crawl. What has changed since 1966? Women are equal now, we're told. We're equal, but a presidential candidate can grab us by the pussy. Men can rape unconscious women as long as they're at a good university. Assault victims who are brave enough to speak up are lying sluts. Over and over again, the message is clear. We deserve it. We deserve it. We deserve it. But we're equal…right?

The amount of women who have felt personally connected to this play is too high. There should not be that many women in the relatively small audiences that a fringe play attracts, knowing exactly what Lucy is going through. Feeling it with her. I didn't write the play, age twenty four, thinking it would ring true with so many women. It breaks my heart. I can barely watch it anymore.

Thank you to Hannah Durose, Pamela Hall, Diana Scrivener, Stephen Myott-Meadows, Mat, Tim and Andy at VAULT Festival, everyone at Underbelly, Chloe Nelkin and her team, Stewart Pringle and the Old Red Lion Theatre, Jean Kitson, Benedict Taylor, Jamie Platt, Justin Nardella, Catherine Morgan, everyone at Samuel French, Emma Thompson and Gaia Wise, Richard Davenport, and Rebecca Pitt.

My Dad is the only proof reader you'll ever need, but he probably won't help you. He has to help me though, because of genetics.

My Mum loves theatre, always has, and she passed that on to me. It means the world when she likes my plays. Thank you Linda Fitzsimons, you are the best mum ever.

This play is as much mine as it is Sarah Meadows', who has been with it since the first messy, weird draft. She is one of the greats, and I'm terrified she will be famous soon and leave me.

Rosalyn Newbery is the best producer in the country, probably the world, possibly the universe.

And without Jessica Butcher, this play wouldn't be still going. So blame her please.

Lastly, a huge thank you to the hundreds of amazing people who have come to see the play so far. It blows my mind every time someone walks in without me dragging them there. Your reactions have meant the world.

Camilla Whitehill
October 2016

For Sarah and Rosalyn

WHERE DO LITTLE BIRDS GO?

A one-woman play

By Camilla Whitehill

SAMUEL FRENCH

samuelfrench.co.uk

Copyright © 2015, 2016 by Camilla Whitehill
All Rights Reserved

WHERE DO LITTLE BIRDS GO? is fully protected under the copyright laws of the British Commonwealth, including Canada, the United States of America, and all other countries of the Copyright Union. All rights, including professional and amateur stage productions, recitation, lecturing, public reading, motion picture, radio broadcasting, television and the rights of translation into foreign languages are strictly reserved.

ISBN 978-0-573-11075-7
www.samuelfrench.co.uk /www.samuelfrench.com
Cover image Rebecca Pitt Creative Ltd

FOR AMATEUR PRODUCTION ENQUIRIES

UNITED KINGDOM AND WORLD EXCLUDING NORTH AMERICA
plays@SamuelFrench-London.co.uk
020 7255 4302/01

Each title is subject to availability from Samuel French, depending upon country of performance.

CAUTION: Professional and amateur producers are hereby warned that WHERE DO LITTLE BIRDS GO? is subject to a licensing fee. Publication of this play does not imply availability for performance. Both amateurs and professionals considering a production are strongly advised to apply to the appropriate agent before starting rehearsals, advertising, or booking a theatre. A licensing fee must be paid whether the title is presented for charity or gain and whether or not admission is charged.

For amateur and professional enquiries please contact Samuel French Ltd, 52 Fitzroy St, London, W1T 5JR.

For first class enquiries please contact Kitson Management Limited, Studio 315 Screenworks, 22 Highbury Grove, London N5 2ER.

No one shall make any changes in this title for the purpose of production. No part of this book may be reproduced, stored in a retrieval system, or transmitted in any form, by any means, now known or yet to be invented, including mechanical, electronic, photocopying, recording, videotaping, or otherwise, without the prior written permission of the publisher. No one shall upload this title, or part of this title, to any social media websites.

The right of Camilla Whitehill to be identified as author of this work has been asserted in accordance with Section 77 of the Copyright, Designs and Patents Act 1988.

USE OF COPYRIGHT MUSIC

A licence issued by Samuel French Ltd to perform this play does not include permission to use any music specified in this copy. Where the place of performance is already licensed by the PERFORMING RIGHT SOCIETY a return of the music used must be made to them. If the place of performance is not so licensed then application should be made to the Performing Right Society, 29 Berners Street, London W1T 3AB. Before your performance please make sure you are adhering to the UK copyright laws.

A separate and additional licence from PHONOGRAPHIC PERFORMANCES LTD, 1 Upper James Street, London W1R 3HG is needed whenever commercial recordings are used.

'Where Do Little Birds Go' Words and Music by Lionel Bart
© 1959, Reproduced by permission of Peter Maurice Music Co Ltd/ EMI Music Publishing Ltd, London W1F 9LD

'For Emily, Whenever I May Find Her'
Copyright © 1966, 1967 Paul Simon (BMI)
International Copyright Secured. All Rights Reserved.
Reprinted by Permission.

God Only Knows
Words and Music by Brian Wilson and Tony Asher
Copyright (c) 1966 IRVING MUSIC, INC.
Copyright Renewed
All Rights Reserved Used by Permission
Reprinted by Permission of Hal Leonard Corporation

**This text is from the original production,
so may differ to what is presented on stage**

CHARACTER
Lucy Fuller
A 24-year-old girl from Hastings, who currently resides in Whitechapel, East London. She spends much of the play recalling events that happened to her age 17/18.

TIME
A winter evening in 1972.

PLACE
Winston's Nightclub in Mayfair.

"I am no bird; and no net ensnares me: I am a free human being with an independent will."
– Charlotte Bronte, *Jane Eyre*.

"I have got no regrets, my brother didn't have any either."
– Reggie Kray in an interview with
The Independent, March 1995

A dark stage. A dressing table with a mirror, and a bigger table with a decanter of whiskey and a glass, a chair. A girl, **LUCY FULLER***, walks on. She is wearing a long men's mackintosh, wrapped around her, a necklace with a wedding ring on it, and no shoes. She regards the audience, then clicks her fingers. The backing track to* Bells Will Ring *from* Charlie Girl *begins to play. She starts to sing as the lights come up.*

She sings the song at the top of her voice. She throws her arms out on the last note and sings it like she's in a West End musical. At the end, we hear applause. **LUCY** *smiles widely, bowing and waving. She waits until it dies down entirely.*

On my 18th birthday my Uncle Keith took me to see *Charlie Girl*, starring the one and only Joe Brown, who I was in love with and was very much hoping to marry. As I sat in the audience, I realised that I was experiencing something I'd never felt before. I was home. I had found my home. I needed to get onto that stage as fast I could. And I told everyone that would listen that I was going to be a West End leading lady. I talked about it at work every day until somebody heard me.

Beat.

My name is Lucy Fuller. I'm 24 and I live in Whitechapel. When I was 18 I was kidnapped by the Kray twins, and locked in a flat with an escaped murderer.

She goes and stands behind the bar, cleaning an invisible glass, doing other activities one would do working at a pub.

I worked at the Blind Beggar on Vallance Road. It was a big old boozer – a dark, thick with smoke, dirt floor sort of place. The manager was a stringy looking fella named Alfie. I was 17. Alfie didn't ask my age when he hired me. Never did, wasn't bothered. Uncle Keith didn't like me working there. I can see now that the idea of your 17-year-old niece working at the pub where Ronnie Kray had recently shot someone in the face wasn't the best, but I dug my heels in, said I was doing it whether he wanted me to or not. He'd decided, as a compromise, that he'd have to come and pick me up from work every night. I said, "I don't need you to do that Uncle Keith, I can look after myself, I have really sharp teeth". Working there, I had to learn who was enemies with who, who'd stolen who's bird, and make sure they were kept apart as much as possible. Honestly, I found the whole thing exciting. I used to walk home with Uncle Keith, asking him what different slang meant. Hampton Wick – prick. Borasic – borasic lint – skint. It was nice. I liked it.

She stops what she's doing. The Charlie Girl Waltz *starts to play very quietly.*

Here, you've all seen a photo of the Krays, haven't you? That famous one with Ronnie all big in the front and Reggie peeking over his shoulder. I have it here somewhere.

She searches her pockets. It's not there.

Beat.

The music gets louder. She smiles, puts her arms around an invisible partner, and starts to waltz on the spot. She speaks as she dances – the music stays on, but low.

I moved up here when I was 17. Followed a boyfriend here. He was a right tosser, really nasty, but you know what it's like when you're 17. He's lovely when it's just me and him! I barely notice his temper! No, this bruise is from rollerskating! D'you know, I found out the other day, he's doing time now. For armed robbery. What a tit. Tommy Bennett, his name was. Dumped him as soon as I got to Charing Cross. He started harping on about how I was dressed, calling me a slapper, so I bit him on the hand.

She mimes biting.

I'm a biter. Not like, sexually, that's just how I defend myself. I bite. So I bit him hard on the hand and legged it.

She does a spin with her invisible partner.

I didn't know anything about London. Mum'd been surprised, I think, that I was leaving. Convinced I was just talking, you know, teenage stuff. But there we were at Hastings Station, and I'd bought my ticket, and I was going. Dad hadn't come to see me off. Mum walked me up to the station to meet Tommy, and when we got there she handed me a fiver and her sister June's address.

"Mum, you said June was a two faced slapper."

"Well she is", said Mum, "but she's got a roof over her head".

She was looking at Tommy, who was scowling at us from the entrance of the station. I told Mum not to worry, that I was gonna become a famous singer. Or a barmaid.

The music comes right up. She goes off waltzing around the space, doing little spins and steps. As the music swells her movements become less strict, she starts to throw herself about the room, leaping and twisting. The music comes to an end. She bows to the invisible partner.

I was in London, on my own, with three mini-skirts and a fiver to my name. I knew June lived in the East End, so I bought myself one of them little A-Z maps and figured out how to get there. One bus, and one long walk later, I was standing outside 27 Vallance Road. It was freezing and getting dark. I'd only met Auntie

June once, when I was little, and all I remembered of her was that she smelt like antiseptic. But she was my only choice, so I knocked on the door. Knocked again. And again.

She stands, coat wrapped around her, shivering and waiting. Waits. And waits.

Ten minutes later I was still on the doorstep. I was about to give up when from right behind me someone went: "Who the hell are you?!"

LUCY *jumps and spins round.*

This huge fella was standing there glaring at me. He looked like a fairytale villain – massive, dark hair and wild eyes. He was clutching a brown bag that was dripping grease.

Unless Auntie June'd undergone some serious changes, this wasn't her.

"Oh, hello, I'm Lucy. I'm looking for June Fitzsimons, she's my Auntie. Does she live here?"

And the oddest thing happened. This giant bloke sort of shrank. He looked like he was going to cry. He said – "I'm Keith, June's husband. Well... ex-husband."

And he looked so pathetic and sad and I felt awful.

Especially awful cause June weren't there and I didn't have anywhere to stay.

"I'm so sorry, my Mum gave me this address for if I was in trouble, I didn't mean to bother you."

"What trouble're you in?"

"I just got up here today, and I don't have any money or a job and I just broke up with my fella, and I'm in a right two-and-eight."

I'd just heard that phrase on the bus. Thought it'd endear me to Keith if I used some of the local lingo. And he let me in.

Keith was the best and nicest man I've ever met or will ever meet. He gave me a home within 30 minutes of meeting me. Still don't know why he did it. He had one son, Jimmy, who was behind bars, and with June gone it was just him. Told me I could stay, if I paid rent. Told me to call him Uncle Keith.

I promised him I'd get a job. I really wanted to be a barmaid, you know, until I became a famous singer. I just had it in my head that being a barmaid would be the second best job ever. I'd worked in a tea rooms back home in Hastings, and that'd been shit and boring, because NOTHING happens in a tea rooms. EVER. Time slows down, actually, because everyone just really quietly sips tea and nibbles scones and all you can hear is the chink of china and I honestly used to go a bit barmy, I used to pretend I was in this competition where I had to use as many doilies as I could, so I just covered people's trays in doilies, I'd write their bill on a doily, eventually I fixed one to my head with hair grips like a fancy hat and that's when my stupid boss Eileen fired me. But pubs are fun, and noisy, people talk to each other. I wanted people to talk to me.

(as Keith) "Be careful, Lucy, some of these pubs have a reputation. The Kray twins were brought up on this very road."

(back to herself) I didn't know who that was.

She goes to the table and gets out a newspaper. She reads from it.

Ronnie and Reggie Kray. Born 24th October 1933.

The kings of organised crime.

She stands, and comes to the front of the stage.

Ronnie once shot a man in the head in broad daylight.

Turned out Uncle Keith'd known them since he was little. Used to do the odd 'job' for them. He worked down the docks after that, but it sounded like June hadn't been happy with his involvement with them. Poor Keith, he was a good bloke. You can see how fellas fall into that, living somewhere like the East End where everyone's ducking and diving. It's normal.

She returns to her bar and carries on with her 'tasks' again.

The Krays didn't look much alike, by the time I met them anyway. I mean, their colouring and that was the same, but Ronnie was much bigger, much scarier looking. Reggie could pass for attractive sometimes.

Pause. **LUCY** *looks up.*

That day in the pub, the day I first saw them, they were dressed identically. Dark wool coats, smart hats. The whole pub went quiet.

LUCY *stops what she's doing and stands completely still. She watches them enter. When she speaks, she does so quietly.*

They wanted to know who I was, what'd happened to 'Rita'. I hadn't heard her mentioned before.

She goes back to what she was doing, slowly, deliberately. She doesn't take her eyes off them.

End of the night they were still there, knocking back gin, when Uncle Keith came in to pick me up. His eyes went all big when he saw the twins sitting there. Reggie approached him, asked him how he'd been. Said he'd heard "your missus ran off with Eddie Sharper". And "should he send someone round to have a word with Eddie". Keith seemed alarmed, told him it was kind to offer but no, that wouldn't be necessary, and got me out of there as quick as he could.

She comes out from behind the bar.

Keith didn't want me working at the Beggar after that. But I told him I didn't care what he said. I liked it there.

Piano starts to play. She jumps up on the bar. She sings a verse of In My Life *by* The Beatles. *She finishes singing, does a little curtsy. She pours herself a drink and sips at it.*

I love singing. I'll sing anywhere and to anyone. I'd sing behind the bar at the Beggar. Or on top of it. I sing in the dressing room at Winston's – I'll tell you about Winston's in a minute. I'd sing to Uncle Keith. I'd sing to Frank –

She stops herself, surprised at her own admission.

He was very sensitive, was Frank. He liked my singing.

She doesn't elaborate. She jumps back behind her bar.

The day after my 18th birthday – when I'd seen *Charlie Girl* – I was belting out the songs behind the bar, annoying Alfie and everyone who came in too. People don't actually like it when their barmaid sings. *Oliver!* is very misleading, Nancy would have been told to shut up with her oom-pah-pahs. Anyway, I was singing and going on to Alfie – "I'd look brilliant in one of them dancer's outfits Alfie. They're really skimpy but classy, and under the lights they look –"

She jumps and turns.

Reggie Kray had tapped me on the shoulder.

LUCY *shuffles forward, nervously.*

He had an offer for me. He said he had friends at Winston's, a famous nightclub in Mayfair. He said they had a space open for a new hostess, and that loads of important theatre people went there. And that sometimes the hostesses were promoted to show girls, and then they'd do dances and cabarets, and that's how loads of girls got started. Barbara Windsor even worked there.

Two days later, I went off on the bus to town to meet Billy Howard, Reggie's 'connection' at Winston's. I met him at the club itself. It was really nice inside – grand, you know. Especially compared to the Beggar. Sometimes the Beggar would just smell like piss for no reason. Even if you'd cleaned the toilets 'til they shone, the piss smell would still hang in the air.

I was expecting an audition of some kind, so I'd prepared a song.

A spotlight suddenly hits **LUCY**. *Music starts to play softly in the background. She smiles widely and starts to sing* Where Do Little Birds Go? *from* Fings Ain't Wot They Used To Be.

WHERE DO LITTLE BIRDS GO TO IN THE
  WINTER TIME?
THERE'LL BE BLIZZARDS AND SNOW TOO IN
  THE WINTER TIME
AND THE THOUGHT OF IT HORRIFIES ME/

The music cuts, lights snap up. Billy has told her to stop singing.

Billy just looked at me and said I had the job. I had to tell him my measurements and that was it, I was a nightclub hostess! I was over the moon. I couldn't believe it had been so easy. Things were just falling into my lap.

What were you doing when you were 18? I was working at a famous nightclub, surrounded by celebrities and beautiful people. I had money to buy records and lipstick, and I lived with my Uncle, who I loved. I was having the time of my life.

The Charlie Girl Waltz *starts up again. She does a few steps, twirls, and comes to a stop as the music fades back down.*

I started at Winston's three days later. Keith had decided to borrow his mate Bob's car every night, so he could come and pick me up. I'd tried to tell him I'd get home on my own, but he wouldn't hear about it. He was still off with me about the job.

She pauses for a moment, goes to say something, then stops.

Back to my first day. I got there, and it was all dark, you know, pre-opening. This girl was sitting at a table, fag hanging out her mouth, reading a magazine. She was Suzy, the head hostess. Suzy doesn't beat around the bush. She looked me up and down, mumbled something about getting ready, then shoved me into the dressing room and left. Inside, a dozen girls were getting themselves ready. The uniforms were even skimpier than I'd anticipated. They were miniscule.

She takes off her coat. She is wearing a skimpy costume.

Are miniscule.

She carefully drapes the coat on the back of a chair.

I was also given a pair of painfully high heels.

From a box or suitcase on one of the tables, she takes out some heels and puts them on.

At the dressing table there were powders and creams and pencils of every colour, and the girls were just whacking them all on their face with abandon.

Out of the box she gets foundation powder and starts applying it in the mirror.

I started applying some vaguely skin-coloured stuff to my face, when a girl with bright yellow hair stopped me. Her name was Val. She became my best friend.

We're still close, we just don't see a lot of each other. She's married to a military bloke and they travel a lot. We write to each other, though. It's nice. I've never had a penpal before.

A pause. She looks back in the mirror and starts putting lipstick on.

Val helped me with my make-up, and helped me get my hair up into a massive beehive, and by the time Suzy returned, I was deemed acceptable. Suzy took me aside.

(She stands, in an impression of Suzy) "You're a hostess. You host. You're there to make the clients happy. You'll be given certain tables, and your job is to make those tables feel special. The blokes at the tables, I mean, not the tables themselves. Sit on their laps, laugh at their jokes, do whatever you can to make them feel like the dishiest bloke in the room. Anything after-hours is up to you to sort out, that isn't our business."

She pours herself another drink, and sits with it.

That was the first I'd heard of "afters". What some of the girls did when the club closed. With certain blokes who frequented it. I didn't know what Suzy was on about, I thought she was referring to a cleaning schedule or something.

Suzy told me to stick with Val for the night, see how things were done. We were sent to a table of three American blokes. I loved their accents, I thought they were the most exotic people I'd ever met, and had a lovely night chatting them up. I couldn't believe this was really a job. If I'd been at the Beggar, I'd have been trying to avoid the advances of a smelly alcoholic. Instead, I was sat on a velvet sofa, necking cocktails and having a giggle.

The Americans stayed all night, and as the club was closing, one of them slid across to me. He whispered in my ear, "How about you come back to my hotel room? I can make it worth your while. What do you say, a hundred for the night?"

She spits out her drink and screams "FUCK OFF".

That caused a ruckus.

I had blokes trying it on all the time at the Beggar. But nobody had ever mistaken me for a... well, a... before. I was shocked. The Yank had leapt up, cursing me at the top of his voice. Val was half laughing, half narked off. She dragged me off the club floor and gave me a right talking to.

LUCY *is dragged away, but not before she snaps her teeth at the men, a mid-air bite.*

"Lucy, you don't have to do anything you don't want to do, but a lot of us do it. It's common knowledge. You can't smack a guy for trying."

But.

It's not nice. For people to make presumptions like that about you.

It was hard, Val said, living on just a hostess salary, if you had no family or nothing to depend on. So she did the "afters". She said, she only went with really rich blokes, who had grand hotel rooms and hot breakfasts in the morning. But I thought, no. That'll never be me. I didn't need any more money and I certainly didn't want to do THAT to get it. And that was fine, for a few months. I went to work, I came home. Keith stopped being off with me. We'd go on long walks through Victoria Park on Sundays. Me and Val started hanging out in the week, going to the flicks and that. Til one day, in early September.

LUCY *stops herself. She suddenly looks very tired. She casts about for what to say.*

(Singing) WHERE DO LITTLE BIRDS GO IN THE
   WINTER TIME?

Pause.

It's Barbara Windsor, that. In *Fings Ain't Wot They Used To Be*. Uncle Keith got me the record for Christmas when I was 17.

Pause. She remembers something.

That first Christmas in London, when I'd only been there a couple of months and I was still at the Blind Beggar, me and Keith had Christmas together, just us two. I worked at the pub in the morning and when I got home, he surprised me with a proper slap up dinner he'd cooked all on his own. We had ham, and potatoes, and veggies, and even a bit of smoked salmon his boss'd given him. It was great. Christmas back home had been a different story. Dad would roll in pissed at about noon, smack Mum about with a nearby serving spoon, then pass out. We'd have to tiptoe around, whispering, eating in silence, ignoring Mum's tears as she carved the meat. I'd always dreaded the day. Not that year.

Pause.

(Singing) THERE'LL BE BLIZZARDS AND SNOW TOO IN THE WINTER TIME.

Pause.

On the 5th September 1966 I came out of work and Uncle Keith wasn't there and he was never late so Val gave me a lift home and I waited up all night for Keith to come home and the police came round in the morning and Keith wasn't with them and Keith had been killed in a car crash on the way to pick me up and I was still wearing my uniform so I looked like a tart and the police officer was very pale and had a posh accent I think it was his first time giving bad news but I didn't cry I just said thank you so really he had it easy I bet some people cry and cry and scream and that would be worse and the other driver had been blind drunk coming home from a nightclub, maybe my nightclub where I worked and Keith had been coming to pick me up even though he hated me doing that job he came every night.

She tugs at her necklace.

He had this on him and nothing else. His wedding ring. Bless him, he never took it off even after June left. I'd tease him about it, try and get him to get rid of it, throw in the Thames or something, move on and find a new lady, cause he was a catch, Uncle Keith. Not many people came to the funeral.

His Dad came up from the country, where he'd moved to, and organised it, and it was me and him, and Alfie and his wife, and a couple of men from the pub, and at the very back, away from the rest of us, amongst the graves, were the Krays. Silent and unmoving, like a pair of crows. Afterwards we went to the Beggar.

Piano starts to play – I'll Never Find Another You *by* The Seekers. *She picks up her drink again and stands to sing. She struggles through the song. One verse before the end, the piano stops playing. She sings the rest unaccompanied, raising her glass in a toast.*

She finishes singing and cries, lost and alone on stage. After a moment, she calms down, and takes a seat.

Uncle Keith had been very generous in how much rent he'd asked me to pay. The amount for the whole house was about three times what I was used to.

Then there was groceries, and little things I hadn't even thought of, soap and that, you never think about buying soap and that until you have to. It costs money! I wouldn't be able to survive on my hostess money. I knew that. But I didn't want to move out of the house, it was too... it had all our stuff in it, I'd added loads of bits I'd found at the second-hand shop, rugs and throws and paintings and I hate moving house. I figured out, if I earnt a little bit more, I could afford about half the rent.

She gets a tissue and fixes her make up in the mirror.

When I went back to work, I put up an ad for a housemate. Luckily, it was Val who answered it. Her fella'd just kicked her out, and she needed a new place.

I went and asked Billy Howard if I could audition to be one of the showgirls, on account of my financial situation, but he said they didn't earn much more than us anyway. He told me to do some "afters".

She stands up, inspecting her outfit.

I asked Val what it was like to go on the game. She said if you weren't a virgin, then it wasn't even an issue.

She smiles bravely at the audience.

Val said she'd never had a bad experience.

She said they were all fancy blokes, the ones from Winston's, and it paid amazingly. Sometimes you'd get repeat customers and they bought you things, furs and jewellery.

Out of the box on the table she gets a fur stole. She wraps it around her shoulders, significantly.

I said I'd never do it. But I never thought I'd be 18 and alone. No parents I could just run back to. No Uncle Keith. No no-one.

She bares her teeth.

I can look after myself.

She stops for a moment – looks at herself in the mirror, uncertain. Then she forges on.

I followed Val's rules: had to be a hotel room, they had to pay for a cab home, no anal or oral, and I had to tell Val where I was going. It was all suprisingly easy, like how I imagine it feels the moment you decide to jump off a cliff. You panic, but you get there, and it's all right, so you just jump. I'd go home the next day and count my money with Val, I'd ignore Keith's face popping up in my brain, or my Mum's. I hadn't spoken to my Mum for a long time.

She returns to the dressing table and adds more make up – lipstick, perfume – and maybe some jewellery – over the next speech. Get Ready *by* The Temptations *plays – loud, then quiet as she speaks.*

Me and Val would go out in the days, splashing our newly found cash, getting our hair set, nails done, you know. It was easy! As much as those rich businessmen whisper to you about "going all night" and "really giving it to you", they actually just want to quietly do it for a couple of minutes then cry about their far away wife. Pathetic, really.

She jumps up and goes to lie on the bar, seductively. She lies on her back, then flips over, smoothly, up onto all fours. She does this, flirty, over the next speech.

Celebrities came into the bar a lot. I can't really name names. Val and me had a little competition going, who could hook the most famous bloke. She won. A certain Welsh popstar. I won't say more than that. And I had a lovely regular named Bernie who would see me a few times a week. He had a beautiful penthouse flat on Park Lane, and it was like having a boyfriend with none of the hassle, and you'd get some cash in the morning.

LUCY *pauses. The music fades away. She strokes her fur.*

It was okay, you know. I didn't mind it. I barely thought about it really.

She takes a deep breath. She hums under her breath and fiddles with her uniform. What's coming up makes her anxious.

She pours a bit more to drink and downs it.

It was December 1966 when I was told Reggie had come to talk to me. I'd spent the day with Val. We were in our favourite caff, Monty's, reading the papers. Val's easily scared and she was on about this escaped criminal, Frank Mitchell. The papers'd nicknamed him 'The Mad Axeman', and Val wanted to get more locks put on the door.

(To Val) "Val, he disappeared in Devon or somewhere, he's hardly gonna show up in East London."

Later on I went to work as usual. It was a normal night. A few gangsters in, couple of European millionaires.

It was about 8 o'clock when I was told about Reggie. I was taken over to his booth in the corner. He was with Tommy Cowley, the fella who 'took care' of the club on behalf of the Krays. Reggie said he had a favour to ask. He had a friend who wanted to meet me. He was an Arab businessman, who was in town for work, and would I come and meet him?

"Do you like Arabs, Lucy?" He said.

"If they're rich."

"My friend is very, very rich. Would you come with us, and keep him company?"

I really didn't want to go. I hated the idea of going with a bloke outside of the club. But say no to Reggie Kray...

So I went. I nearly asked for the money upfront, but... we all got into a waiting car, and started to drive.

She takes a chair to the front of the stage and sits as if she's squashed between two people.

I was wedged next to Tommy Cowley who stank of old smoke and sweat. I expected this bloke to be in a hotel nearby, but after ten minutes I realised we were out of the West End and heading East. When we got to Limehouse I started to worry. I asked where we were going, but Tommy Cowley "shh"-d me. It was getting dark and, as we drove further, I lost my bearings. I didn't know where I was, and I realised, I hadn't told Val where I was going. Everyone was so quiet.

Eventually, we pulled up in front of this dingy looking block of flats, and I was led to the front door.

She stands as if being pulled by the arm.

Tommy knocked twice, then waited. The curtains twitched next to us, and the door was opened a crack. A slim, good looking fella peered out at us, then opened the door proper to let us in. Inside was boiling and airless, a grim little shithole of a flat, dirty carpet and the smell of body odour hanging in the air. In short, not a place you'd generally find a wealthy Arab businessman. I'm not sure how keen they are on nasty flats in Barking. There was me, Reggie, Tommy, this bloke who'd answered the door, and a hunched figure in an armchair in the corner, smoking a fag like it was his last. His name was Exley, I was told, and the bloke who answered the door was Albert Donoghue. Everyone just kind of stood there for a minute. Then, from a room off the living area, a huge brick wall of a man entered. Taller than everyone else by a head, and twice as wide, he seemed to fill the entire space. I clocked his face and had to grab onto the wall to stop from properly collapsing.

Pause.

It was Frank Mitchell.

All I could think of was how funny, Val was right, he's in East London! And then it hit me that I would probably die in that room. Which was less funny.

She stands as if she is back there, staring up at this huge man.

He was looking at me in a very strange way, not a murder-y way, but sort of desperate. I decided that if I was going to be killed, I'd have been killed by then. So I turned to Reggie.

She spins on her heel and faces him.

Where's my money? I want my money upfront. You want me to do a job, you better pay me.

She stares down the invisible Reggie.

He didn't want to do what I said but he was so shocked he just did. He went off with Tommy to get my cash, which they didn't have with them. I suppose they thought Reggie Kray gets these sorts of things for free.

She sits, waiting. A moment passes.

Eventually, Tommy and Reggie came back with a hundred quid, 20 of which Albert took for 'expenses'. That whole time, Frank had just stood quietly across the room from me, looking like a little boy stuck in a giant's body. When I'd got my money, I stood up and went – "come on then."

Music starts to play – For Emily, Wherever I May Find Her *by* Simon & Garfunkel.

LUCY *slowly takes off her fur stole and puts it back on the box. She takes off her heels and puts them back in the box. She takes off her stockings, carefully, and puts them in the box.*

She goes and lies down on the table, on her back, with her legs apart. She lies there still. She turns over onto her front.

She moves up onto all fours, then back onto her knees to speak.

It was very heavy going. He would go at it hard, fast, no rhythm change. He'd do it until he finished, then he'd spring onto the floor, where he'd do 50 push ups. Then he'd get back on the bed and start again.

She repeats the movements from before.

It went on for hours.

She repeats the same sequence again. The music fades to silence.

It must have been about 4 in the morning when he fell asleep. He curled up on the floor like a dog. I stayed perched on the bed. Feeling...

She turns so her legs are hanging off the table.

It was very hard. It was a very bad night. I was 18.

She stays there for a moment. Then she gets off the table, shivering a bit – she's cold. She gets the chair, and carries it, on tip-toes, to the front of the stage, trying to be quiet. Over this:

The next morning, I snuck into the kitchen, where Exley made me fried eggs. We ate them in silence.

She sits on the chair, looking around nervously. A door bell rings. She looks up.

At about nine, Reggie came round. He made the others leave so he could have a 'word' with me. Basically to tell me I was up shit creek without a paddle. Reggie and Ronnie had broken Frank out of prison and had hoped to get round the authorities somehow – really clever plan – but they weren't particularly interested in helping an escaped criminal. He told me, "this is like the war. You're in it for the duration." He didn't care. Him and Ronnie had no real human feeling, you know? Except for their beloved mother.

She watches Reggie leave. She sits alone.

I knew I'd be lucky to get out of this alive. Or to see Val and the girls, or my Mum, ever again. I knew too much, see. I knew what the Krays did to people they needed to disappear.

She looks up.

I looked at the tiny, fogged up windows, sunlight straining against the murky glass, and thought – if only I could climb out of them and fly away. Fly so high that nobody could catch me. Fly until I couldn't see the ground.

Boots of Spanish Leather *by* Bob Dylan *starts to play. She starts, as if there's someone there. She nods, and reluctantly goes back to the table, where she goes through the movement sequence again a few times.*

At the end, she moves to the end of the 'bed', and looks at the man sitting next to her. The music fades down.

Afterwards, Frank dressed himself and sat at the end of the bed, looking at me. We'd barely exchanged a word to each other up to that point. He told me he thought I was beautiful, asked about where I came from. I said I lived near the Krays, actually, and that made him start waxing lyrical about Ronnie.

"Ronnie's my best friend, he's a diamond, he got me out of Dartmoor."

Well where was he then? Frank admitted he hadn't been to see him, but Ronnie'd promised he'd take Frank down to his house in the country. He asked me if I liked the country.

(As if to Frank:) "It's all right."

He made me promise I'd come with him when he went. Said we'd have the most lovely time. He spoke about it a lot. Our holiday to the country. It was boring there, boring and terrifying. All we did was fuck and talk, fuck and talk.

She moves about, bored and frustrated. Looks in boxes, pours another drink, paces about.

And not in the way you would with a new lover. Nothing like that. That's when I started singing to him. Stopped him talking. Calmed him down. Sometimes it would send him to sleep, which was handy.

She goes to the bed and faces Frank. Softly at first, she sings God Only Knows *by* The Beach Boys*:*

I MAY NOT ALWAYS LOVE YOU
BUT LONG AS THERE ARE STARS ABOVE YOU
YOU NEVER NEED TO DOUBT IT
I'LL MAKE YOU SO SURE ABOUT IT

GOD ONLY KNOWS WHAT I'D BE WITHOUT YOU

Frank is asleep. She moves off the bed and sings to the audience .

IF YOU SHOULD EVER LEAVE ME
THOUGH LIFE WOULD STILL GO ON BELIEVE ME
THE WORLD COULD SHOW NOTHING TO ME
SO WHAT GOOD WOULD LIVING DO ME

She stops, the last line sinking in.

GOD ONLY KNOWS WHAT I'D BE WITHOUT YOU.
GOD ONLY KNOWS WHAT I'D BE WITHOUT YOU.
GOD ONLY KNOWS WHAT I'D BE...

A change of mood. It is the next day.

There was a moment of excitement the following day, when *The Times* and *The Mirror* published Frank's letters. Frank and Albert had written these silly letters to the newspapers, asking for understanding and help. *The Mirror* added a comment – "Wherever you are, Frank, be a man and give yourself up". That really upset Frank. By that point, that's what he wanted to do – give himself in. When Reggie came over later that day, Frank suggested that he just give himself in and end the whole sorry mess. Reggie wasn't happy. He made it clear to Frank that that would happen over everyone's dead bodies.

Frank had exchanged one prison for another.

And to be fair, the little flat was worse than Dartmoor. He told me he'd actually been allowed out, when he was there. He even made it to the pub from time to time. Didn't give me much faith in the prison system, but I could see his frustration now. Locked in a shitty flat with two gangsters and a nightclub hostess. It was like a sitcom, but not funny. At all. The publication of his letters made no difference – there was no contact, no news from anybody. The plan hadn't worked. We all sat in that dark, stuffy little flat, waiting for something to happen. Occasionally punctuated by humping. I thought, if this is how I die, please God don't let my Mum find out the details.

She curls up on the floor, with a drink.

The atmosphere in the flat grew tenser by the minute. Albert would pace up and down; Exley would crack his knuckles incessantly. Frank buzzed with barely contained frustration, and I couldn't think of anything to do except try and keep him calm.

(*Sings*) WHAT'LL BECOME OF ALL THOSE LITTLE LARKS
NOW THERE IS NO MORE NESTING IN THE PARKS?

It felt like we were keeping an eagle in a canary's cage.

He was just miserable.

She gets up, approaches Frank.

AND WHEN YOU RAN TO ME
YOUR CHEEKS FLUSHED WITH THE NIGHT.
WE WALKED ON FROSTED FIELDS OF JUNIPER AND LAMPLIGHT,
I HELD YOUR HAND.

She has calmed him down.

I knew Frank was a dangerous bloke – I'd read the papers. That being said, he was never violent to me. He seemed to genuinely like having me there.

She leaves Frank – perhaps he is asleep.

Frank talked obsessively about Ronnie.

He'd ask Albert where he was constantly. He'd sit for hours, watching out for him through a crack in the curtains. "Where is he? Why hasn't he visited? I thought he was my friend".

I couldn't help but think, oh Frank. Men like the Kray twins don't have friends.

She returns to the bed.

That night Frank climbed onto the bed next to me after his last set of press ups. He told me that I was the only one he could trust. That I was the only honest person he knew. Then he said – he said "... I think I love you, Lucy."

She faces Frank, a look of surprise and fear on her face. To us.

Fancy that. The first man to ever tell me he loved me, and he was an escaped murderer that I'd been locked in a flat with.

She nods, taking it in, then says -

"I love you too, Frank."

She looks at us.

What was I meant to say? I felt sorry for him.

After a pause she hops off the bed. Puts down her drink. Starts to pace.

Next morning, Frank woke up angry. He asked me to help him write a note to Ron. I didn't want to be involved with it but I felt I couldn't say no. He wrote that unless something was done soon, he'd go round to Vallance Road and 'visit' their mother. He gave it to Albert to pass on. Any idiot could see that was a barmy idea. We all sat around waiting for the response.

It came quickly. The next morning a note was sent round. Albert told Frank the news, that Ronnie was down in the country and he wanted Frank to join him for Christmas. To avoid arousing any suspicions, an unmarked van would come round and collect Frank and himself that evening, at six o'clock. Ron "sent his love", apparently. He "couldn't wait to see his old friend Frank".

It had to be a trap. I felt wretched. But, at the end of the day, he couldn't stay there.

The waiting was unbearable.

Frank was buzzing around the flat, so excited, talking about his friend Ronnie, and how he'd come through for him after all. Telling me how much he loved me, how excited he was to spend Christmas with me, how God himself must've sent me down from heaven.

She hastily pours herself another drink.

By five o'clock, Albert had started explaining to Frank why I wouldn't be joining him in the van.

(As Albert:) "Frank, mate, she can't go with you. Imagine what would happen to her if you were stopped by the pigs? Lucy will come on later. That all right?"

And Frank believed him, he believed all the nonsense. He believed that notorious criminal Ronnie Kray was down in the country with his Mum decorating a Christmas tree and cooking a ham for his arrival. I mean, Frank was mentally ill, you know? It was like abuse. It was abuse. And Albert said all this so easily, so smoothly. I hated him. A minute later, Frank took me into the little room and handed me a Christmas card. He'd had someone go out and buy it for him.

She goes to the box and gets out a Christmas card.

Inside it said, "For Lucy, the only one I love." I stared at that card and felt sick. His handwriting was like a toddler's.

She traces the writing with her fingertips.

I kissed him, for the last time. I thought, when it's all done, maybe I'd go visit him in Dartmoor. When he'd calmed down or what have you. If the Krays let me leave. We went out into the living area. There were a few fellas there by that time, more of the Kray's men. Exley peaked out the curtains and nodded at Albert. Everyone said, "Happy Christmas, Frank". "Enjoy yourself, Frank".

LUCY *watches Frank leave. She lifts one hand up and waves goodbye, a fixed smile on her face. Once he leaves, she breathes a sigh of relief.*

She smiles to herself – it's over. She closes her eyes and sings quietly.

WHERE DO LITTLE BIRDS GO IN THE WINTER TIME?
THERE'LL BE BLIZZARDS AND SNOW TOO IN THE/

She is cut off by the piercing sound of gun shots. 18 in total rapid, one after another. She stares ahead, not moving, as the shots ring out.

Then silence.

It just didn't cross my mind. It just didn't occur to me.

Pause.

I thought they were taking him back to prison. I thought/

Christmas music comes on, interrupting her, loud – too loud. Christmas (Baby please come home) *by Darlene Love.* **LUCY** *is pulled away; confused, scared, she stuffs the Christmas card down her dress. She is pulled over to the chair, she sits in it. The music fades down to a low level.*

They burnt everything in the flat. Pillows, sheets, papers. Then they drove me to a party. A house party in Walthamstow.

The music comes up again. **LUCY** *is pushed into the party. She stands, uncomfortable.*

I ended up in a corner with Albert, who swore he hadn't known what was going to happen to Frank. We drank a bottle of whisky and sat there until the party was over. That's when it all hit me. When it got quiet.

The music has gone. **LUCY** *quietly gets herself a drink.*

Albert comforted me. I went back to his house. As he pushed himself inside me I wondered where Frank was.

I thought he was probably at the bottom of a river, being nibbled by fishes. I hoped he hadn't gone to hell. I mean, I don't believe in all that anyway, but at that moment, I thought – please let me be right, that there's nothing afterwards, that he's just gone to sleep.

Quietly, **LUCY** *goes to get her stockings and shoes, which she puts on. She wraps the fur stole around her neck, then puts the coat on over the top. Over this:*

I went out with Albert for a couple of months after that. I don't know why. He wasn't very nice. I had to use my teeth on him a few times.

The Krays were arrested the next year, and the court case was in 1969, when I was 21. I was brought in as a witness. I didn't want to go, I begged them not to make me. I tried to run away. But the police said I was safe.

I think I'm safe. I think I am.

She goes to leave then stops.

I've got to get to work. I'm still at Winstons.

Pause.

They've said I can sing in the late night shows, if I want.

The backing track from the beginning of the show comes on. She opens her mouth to sing, but nothing comes out.

The music continues.

LUCY *just stands there. Then she leaves without a word.*

End.

Property Plot

Table with a mirror (p1)
A bar (p1)
Decanter with whiskey and a glass (p1)
Several chairs and smaller tables (p1)
Newspaper (p5)
Pours herself a drink and sips it (p7)
Box (may be substituted for a drawer in a table) (p9)
Foundation powder (p9)
Lipstick (p10)
Pours herself a drink (p10)
Tissue (p13)
Fur Stole (p14)
Make-up (p15)
Perfume (p15)
Jewellery (p15)
Stockings (p18)
Boxes (p20)
Christmas card (p24)

Costume:
Lucy : Long men's mackintosh coat (p1)
Necklace with a wedding ring on it (p1)
Skimpy costume (p10)

Sound Effects Plot

Backing track to *Bells Will Ring* from *Charlie Girl* (p1)
The *Charlie Girl Waltz* starts to play (p2)
The *Charlie Girl Waltz* music gets louder (p2)
The *Charlie Girl Waltz* music stays on, but low (p2)
The *Charlie Girl Waltz* music comes right up (p3)
The *Charlie Girl Waltz* music comes to an end (p3)
Piano starts to play (p7)
Song: *Where Do Little Birds Go, Barbara Windsor - Fings Ain't Wot They Used To Be* (p8)
Music stops and lights snap up (p8)
The Charlie Girl Waltz starts up again (p8)

Music fades back down (p8)
Piano starts to play *I'll Never Find Another You* by *The Seekers* (p13)
Piano stops playing (p13)
Get Ready by *The Temptations* plays loud and then quiet (p15)
The music fades away (p15)
Music starts to play: *For Emily, Wherever I May Find Her* by *Simon & Garfunkel* (p18)
The music fades (p18)
Boots of Spanish Leather by *Bob Dylan* plays (p19)
The music fades down (p20)
Music starts to play: *God Only Knows* by *The Beach Boys* (p20)
Sound of gun shots (p25)
Christmas music plays (p25)
Music fades out (p25)
Music comes up (p25)
Music stops (p25)
Backing track from the beginning of the show comes on (p26)

Lighting Plot

Lights up (p1)
Lights snap up (p9)

Blackout (p27)